Eight Even Sillier Plays

Paul Groves

Star Plays
Series Editor: *Roy Blatchford*

Longman

Contents

1 The Bank Raid

Mum forces Louie to take his younger brother and sister with him on the bank raid. Well I know that they are not very bright but she doesn't want them around the house all day.

Characters	Mum
	Louie
	Alf the Snatch
	Jimbo
	Alma, Louie's younger sister
	Girl in shop, Millicent
	Manageress
	Teddie, Louie's younger brother
	Policeman

1 *Louie's house*

Mum   Go on, Louie.

Louie   No, Mum.

Mum   You must take them with you.

Louie   I can't, Mum. What would the boys say?

Mum   You listen to the boys before your own mother?

Louie   It's not that, Mum.

Mum   Well, what is it then?

Louie   You know.

Mum   I don't know.

Louie   Well, let's put it this way: Alma and Teddie didn't get no exams.

Mum   Are you saying they're stupid?

Louie	No, I'm not saying they're stupid, Mum.
Mum	Your own brother and sister and you say they're stupid.
Louie	No, Mum, they haven't got what it takes to do a bank job.
Mum	Alma and Teddie look up to you.
Louie	Don't, Mum.
Mum	You're their hero.
Louie	Don't, Mum.
Mum	If you don't take them with you, you know what I'll do?
Louie	What?
Mum	I'll never cook you another treacle pud.
Louie	Don't say that, Mum.
Mum	Never again.

2 *The old warehouse*

Alf, Louie and Jimbo are deep in conversation

Alf	You're not saying those two dimmies are coming with us on the job?
Louie	They've got to.
Jimbo	Why?
Louie	Me Mum's putting the pressure on.
Alf	But they could ruin it. I mean we gave him a gun that time.
Louie	I'm sorry about your toes, Alf.
Alf	I can never wear sandals again.
Jimbo	She's worse. I mean, she's carrying the loot away when she sees her friend on the other side of the street. What does she do? She drops the bag and goes and has a chat.

Alf	That's not as bad as my toes.
Jimbo	There was ten grand in that bag.
Alf	Are you saying . . .?
Louie	Stop it! Look, I'll give them some simple jobs.
Jimbo	Simple?
Louie	Teddie can get the second car and Alma can go and buy the stockings.
Alf	They'll mess it up.
Louie	Even Alma and Teddie can't get that wrong.

3 *A department store*

Alma approaches a girl assistant, Millicent

Alma	Five stockings, please.
Girl	You mean five pairs, madam.
Alma	They're just five of us.
Girl	Then you want five pairs.
Alma	We only want one each.
Girl	One each? Oh, the poor dears! Have they only got one leg?
Alma	No, we've got two legs.
Girl	Then you need five pairs.
Alma	They're not going on our legs, they're going on our heads.
Girl	Heads? You want the hat department, madam.
Alma	I'm not stupid, I want five stockings.
Girl	What sort do you want?
Alma	Any sort. As long as you can see through them.
Girl	All our stockings show off the leg well, madam.
Alma	Look, it's not me legs, it's me head, are you . . .

Manageress	Leave this customer to me, Millicent. Now what shade would you like, madam?
Alma	I don't want a shade, I want five stockings.
Manageress	We have some nice ones here in red.
Alma	They wouldn't go with me nose.
Manageress	Your nose? What about these yellow ones?
Alma	No, we don't want to be con ... conspic ... conspic-uous, do we? Black will be best.
Manageress	I'm afraid we only have tights in black.
Alma	Oh, they're no good.
Manageress	No good?
Alma	I mean, what would you do with the other leg.

4 *The old warehouse*

Louie and Alf are joined by Alma and Teddie

Louie	What have you got that camera for?
Teddie	Me Mum said I could bring it.
Louie	An instant camera?
Teddie	She said she would like some snaps.
Louie	Snaps! I ask you ...
Alf	Jimbo can't come.
Louie	Can't come?
Alf	His wife says as it's a nice day he's got to take her and the kids to Southend.
Louie	What an outfit! Teddie, you'll have to get all the transport. Get something fast for the first and something nobody will notice for the second.
Teddie	Where do you want the second?
Louie	Woolies' car park.
Teddie	Oh good, I can get some pick an' mix.

Louie	Not today, you fool. Just concentrate on the transport.
Teddie	Right, Louie.
Louie	Now synchronise your watches.
Alma	Sin . . . what?
Alf	Make sure our watches have the same time. I ask you . . .
Louie	Cool it, Alf. It is now nine forty five precisely. Okay, Teddie?
Teddie	Mickey's big hand is on the ten and his little hand is on . . .
Louie	You haven't got your Mickey Mouse watch on?
Teddie	Father Christmas brought it for me.
Alf	Father Christmas . . .!
Louie	Alma, where are the stockings?
Alma	I couldn't get stockings.
Louie	Couldn't get stockings?
Alma	No, I've got these football socks.
Louie	Football socks!
Teddie	Oh good, they're Chelsea ones.
Louie	You can't see through them!
Alf	We'll have to cut holes in them.
Teddie	But that would ruin them.
Louie	Quickly . . .

5 *A car park near the High Street*

Louie, Alma and Alf are waiting. Teddie arrives

Louie	Where's the transport?
Teddie	Here.
Louie	Here?

Teddie	I couldn't get a car so I got a . . .
Louie	Sledge!
Teddie	They're ever so fast. I've seen them on telly. They can do a ton.
Alma	Teddie, there's no snow.
Teddie	No snow, oh.
Alf	Now we'll have to walk.
Alma	Can't we go by bus?
Louie	No we can't.
Teddie	No, they don't stop outside the bank.
Alf	Give me strength!
Louie	I hope you've got some proper wheels in Woolies' car park.
Teddie	Oh, yes, that's all fixed.

6 *Outside the bank*

It has been robbed. Bells are ringing. Alma and Teddie are standing around as Louie comes out of the bank with bags of cash

Louie	Quick!
Teddie	Is that you, Louie?
Louie	Of course it's me.
Teddie	I didn't recognise you in that sock.

Alf charges out from the bank

Alf	Run!
Teddie	Can you just stand by the bags so I can get a good snap?
Alma	I'll have to comb me hair first. Make sure you get me good side.
Alf	For heaven's sake!

Teddie	Can you move to the left? I'm looking right into the sun.
Louie	Come on, you fool.
Teddie	But they take thirty seconds to come out.

7 *Woolworth's car park*

They arrive, running

Louie	*(out of breath)* What on earth's that?
Teddie	An ice cream van.
Alf	An ice cream van!
Teddie	Nobody will notice that.
Alma	But what if somebody stops us for a cornet?
Teddie	We can say we're sold out.
Alma	Oh, you are clever.
Louie	We'll have to make the best of it. Fling in the loot.

8 *On the road*

They have just stopped in their getaway van

Louie	What have you stopped for?
Teddie	That kid just flagged me down.
Alma	There's a queue forming.
Louie	Quick. Get on!

Later. The sound of chimes is heard

Louie	What have you put the chimes on for?
Teddie	I like a bit of music when I'm driving.
Alma	Oh yes, let's have some music.
Alf	But it'll draw attention to us.
Louie	Oh no!

Alf	What is it?
Louie	A patrol car is flashing us to stop.
Alf	We're done for.

They stop. A policeman comes up to the ice cream van

Policeman	Good morning. Could I have a cornetto and a choc ice, please?
Louie	A cornetto and a choc ice, now where did I put them?
Alma	Here they are.
Louie	Good girl. We've just taken over this round.
Policeman	It's a hot day. Well, don't you want anything?
Louie	What?
Policeman	The money.
Teddie	We've plenty of that. We've just . . .
Alf	Eighty p, please.

The policeman hands over a five-pound note

Policeman	Can you change this?
Teddie	Oh, yes, we've bags of it down here.
Policeman	Bags?
Louie	Yes, we've had a busy day. Being so hot.
Policeman	Oh, that's a nice camera. I'm a keen photographer myself.
Teddie	Are you? Then you'd like to see my snaps. Look there's Louie and Alf with Alma with the loot outside the bank.
Policeman	Ha! Ha! You will have your little joke. Cheerio.

9 *Louie's house*

Mum	There, did you have a nice day?
Teddie	Lovely, Mum. I've got some snaps.
Alma	I've come out ever so well.

Mum   Where's Louie?

Teddie   He didn't feel well. He's gone to the doctor's.

Alma   His stomach was playing up.

Mum   He will bolt his food.

Teddie   Look there's a snap of us in the ice cream van.

Mum   His treacle pud will get cold. Let me look. I didn't know our Louie had white hair.

2 The Chemistry Lesson

Are any of your teachers as batty as Dr Batty? No chemistry thingummy has ever been like this!

Characters	Dr Batty
	David Jenkins
	Chris Smith
	Tom Brown
	Sally Winter
	Pamela Perkins
	Anne Dewhurst
	Headmaster

A posh school: chemistry laboratory

Dr Batty, the chemistry teacher, enters

Dr Batty Which class is this?

Jenkins 2B, sir.

Dr Batty Well, go on, finish it.

Jenkins What do you mean, sir?

Dr Batty To be or not to be, that is the question.

Jenkins What's that, sir?

Dr Batty Shakespeare.

Smith But this is a chemistry lesson, sir.

Dr Batty I'm in the wrong classroom then.

Sally No, sir, you're taking us.

Dr Batty Taking you where?

Pamela Nowhere, sir.

Dr Batty I can't take you nowhere. That's not logical. I can take you somewhere. Where shall we go?

Brown	You're taking us for a chemistry lesson here, sir.
Dr Batty	Then why didn't you say so, Jenkins.
Brown	Brown, sir.
Dr Batty	No, I prefer white, especially the crusty sort.
Brown	No, I am Brown, sir.
Dr Batty	Then you've been sitting in the sun too much.
Brown	No, my name is Brown.
Dr Batty	I thought you were Jenkins.
Jenkins	No, I'm Jenkins, sir.
Dr Batty	Right, Jenkins, get out the things.
Jenkins	What things are those?
Dr Batty	Really, boy, the things that do the whatnot.
Jenkins	I don't understand, sir.
Dr Batty	Really, Perkins.
Jenkins	Jenkins, sir.
Dr Batty	Really, Jenkins, how long have you been at this school?
Jenkins	Two years, sir.
Dr Batty	Only two! I've been here . . . *(counting on his fingers)* One, two, three, four, five, six, seven, eight, thingy, ten, er um . . . How do you count after ten?
Anne	You could take a shoe off, sir.
Dr Batty	I'm not going to bed.
Anne	No, to count on your toes.
Dr Batty	What a brilliant idea! You are top of the class, Sally.
Anne	Anne, sir.
Dr Batty	An' what? Go on.
Anne	No, my name is Anne.
Dr Batty	Oh. Yes, I've been here fourteen years. Now why was I counting that up?

Jenkins	You were telling me about the things, sir.
Dr Batty	Ah, the things. Have you got them out?
Sally	We don't know what things you mean, sir.
Dr Batty	How long have you been here?
Sally	Two years, sir.
Dr Batty	Only two! I've been here . . .
Pamela	We've been through that, sir.
Dr Batty	Been through it. Well, that's the end of the lesson then. Goodbye.

He makes for the door

Anne	Come back, sir. We haven't started yet.
Dr Batty	Right, get out your books.
Smith	You left them on the bus, sir.
Dr Batty	Why should I do that?
Brown	You didn't have the fare, sir. You left them with the conductor.
Dr Batty	Ah, yes, now what is the best conductor?
Jenkins	Copper, sir.
Dr Batty	The police! I didn't do it. I swear I am innocent.
Jenkins	No, copper wire.
Dr Batty	Exactly. I never sold it for scrap. I am innocent.
Smith	Then we can get on with the lesson then, sir.
Dr Batty	Right, light up.
Brown	We can't smoke in your lesson, sir.
Dr Batty	No, light up the things.
Pamela	Oh, the bunsen burners, sir.
Dr Batty	That's it, the bunsen burners. Now take out the doofahs.
Sally	Doofahs?
Dr Batty	You know. Do for this and do for that.

Sally	You mean test tubes, sir.
Dr Batty	We're not testing any tubes today. I'm in a rush. No, the doofahs.
Anne	The glass beakers, sir.
Dr Batty	Precisely. Now fill them full of stuff.
Smith	What stuff, sir?
Dr Batty	Really, Brown, the stuff that comes out of the doings.
Smith	Doings, sir?
Pamela	He means tap.
Jenkins	Ah water, sir.
Dr Batty	That's kind of you, but I think I prefer a Coke.
Jenkins	No, I mean fill the beakers full of water.
Dr Batty	That's right, then thingy it.
Anne	Thingy it?
Dr Batty	Oh what is the word?
Brown	Boil, sir.
Dr Batty	Oh have you? Yes, it does look nasty. All red and blotchy.
Smith	That's his face, sir.
Dr Batty	Poor boy. Now put in this stuff.
Jenkins	What stuff, sir?
Dr Batty	This stuff in the thingummybob.
Jenkins	It's brown, sir.
Dr Batty	What's Brown done now? And how dare he!
Jenkins	No, the stuff is brown, sir.
Dr Batty	So it should be. Now put in a bit of it.
Sally	How much, sir?
Dr Batty	Oh, I should think about ten p each.
Sally	No, how much stuff shall I put in?

Dr Batty	Oh a handful or two. Now when the stuff has thingied . . .
Brown	Boiled, sir?
Dr Batty	Yes, I am hot. Open a window.
Jenkins	You mean we boil up the stuff with the water.
Dr Batty	Precisely.
Pamela	It's boiling, sir.
Dr Batty	Ah let me taste it.
Sally	But it's chemicals, sir.
Dr Batty	Delicious. Try it.
Anne	It's coffee!
Dr Batty	Precisely. Just in time for break. All we need now is some white stuff.
Smith	Milk, sir?
Dr Batty	Precisely. Has anybody got a cow with them?

The Headmaster comes in

Headmaster	Ah, Dr Batty. I've good news for you. The Government have been on the phone. They want you to lead a new scientific project. Congratulations.

He goes out

Dr Batty	Who was that?
Smith	The Head, sir.
Dr Batty	No, not just the head, the rest of the body as well.
Jenkins	No, the Headmaster, sir.
Dr Batty	How long's he been here?
Anne	Three years, sir.
Dr Batty	Yes let's have three cheers as you suggest. Hip . . . hip . . . Well, I'm off.

He opens a door and walks into a cupboard. There is a crash of glass.

3 The Case of the Missing Holes

Why have all the holes in London gone missing? And why are all those cats at 221B Baker Street? Read this play and you still won't find out.

Characters	Narrator
	Sherlock Holmes
	Dr Watson
	Woman 1
	Woman 2
	Woman 3
	Man
	Dick Whittington

221B Baker Street

Narrator The scene of our play is 221B Baker Street, the home of that ace sleuth Sherlock Holmes. Outside there is a thick London fog, a real peasouper. Holmes is pacing about with a mirror.

Holmes Ah! Ah! Quick, Watson. Look in this mirror.

Watson It's only me.

Holmes Thank goodness, I thought it was me.

Watson No, it's only me, Holmes.

Holmes Let me look again. God, it *is* me. I have small black things growing from my face. Am I turning into a monster, Watson?

Watson You just need to shave, Holmes. Don't frighten me.

Holmes Ha! I only did it to razor laugh. God, I'm so bored, Watson. We've had no crimes to solve for two days.

Watson	It must be the fog, Holmes. Nobody would venture out in fog like this.
Holmes	Yes. Just think, Watson, out in that fog is lurking Moriarty, that fiend in human shape. He could be creeping up on us now.

The doorbell sounds

Narrator	The doorbell rings. Watson jumps.
Watson	Ah!
Holmes	Don't be a fool, Watson. It's only the door. Answer it.
Watson	But it hasn't spoken to me.
Holmes	I mean open it, you fool.
Watson	How, Holmes?
Holmes	Turn the key in the lock.
Watson	God, you're brilliant, Holmes.
Holmes	Elementary, my dear Watson.
Narrator	Watson opens the door. A distraught woman rushes in. Hair is hanging over her face. So is her nose. She is carrying a cat.
Woman 1	Nursing Homes?
Holmes	Sherlock Holmes.
Woman 1	That must be difficult to say with false teeth.
Holmes	It is.
Woman 1	How unfortunate. Who is this?
Holmes	This is Watson. He's a doctor.
Woman 1	This is my cat. He's been doctored as well.
Holmes	What has brought you here?
Woman 1	A number twenty six bus.
Holmes	No, I mean what mystery do you wish me to unravel? Is the cat a clue?
Woman 1	No, it's a tom. Look at this, Children's Homes.

Watson	A packet of Polo mints. Oh goody!
Woman 1	Look at them closely.
Holmes	God, there are no holes in the middle of them.
Woman 1	Yes ... because ...
	A trumpet fanfare is heard
	... somebody has stolen the holes.
Holmes	What a dastardly deed!
Watson	Nothing surprises me these days, Holmes.
Holmes	You fool, it is nothing that surprises me. Where has nothing gone? You won't be able to get your tongue in the middle.
Watson	We could spend a hole year on this case.
Narrator	A distraught man rushes in.
Man	Mr Holmes, this nut ...
Holmes	I'm not hungry.
Man	No, this nut and bolt. You can't get the bolt in the nut because there is no hole!
Watson	I like whole nut.
Holmes	If it goes on like this, there will soon be no hole in the 'O' of my name.
Watson	Then you won't know who you are.
Holmes	Exactly, Watson. I see Moriarty's hand in this. He wishes to confuse me to cover up some big scheme of treachery.
Narrator	Another distraught woman rushes in. She has wild eyes and a tame cat.
Woman 2	Mr Holmes, the plughole of my bath has disappeared! What shall I do?
Watson	Wash in the kitchen.
Woman 2	I could not sink so low.
Holmes	This is a dirty business. Why have you brought your cat?

Woman 2	I want to tell you nine stories about him.
Holmes	Why?
Woman 2	Because he's a cat o' nine tails.

A fanfare is heard

Watson	But a cat's only got one tail.
Narrator	Yet another distraught woman rushes in. She carries a cat with a blue ribbon round its neck.
Holmes	Why has your cat got a blue ribbon round its neck?
Woman 3	Because she's a Tory cat.
Watson	How do you know she's a Tory cat?
Woman 3	Because she's called Moggie Thatcher.

Another fanfare

	Mr Holmes, the Underground railway has disappeared.
Holmes	Ah! I have a train of thought.
Watson	Yes, Holmes.
Holmes	This could escalate, Watson. Look out of the window.
Watson	The curtains are drawn.
Holmes	Pull them back.
Watson	Brilliant, Holmes. God, 'Moriarty's Cheap Bus Service – fifty pounds a ticket'.
Holmes	And that cab.
Watson	'Moriarty's very fair fare taxi service – two pounds'.
Holmes	And that shop.
Watson	'Moriarty's shoe repair service – twenty pounds a shoe'.
Holmes	Moriarty has cornered London Transport.
Watson	Nobody will be able to get about without paying him vast sums of money.
Holmes	Quick, to the Bahamas.
Watson	Why the Bahamas?

Holmes	I need a holiday away from this fog.
Watson	Don't weaken, Holmes, you must not let Moriarty beat you. You must play him at his own game.
Holmes	Does he play snooker? I could pot the blackguard.
Watson	No, you must solve the mystery of the missing holes.
Holmes	I'll have to go underground to beat him.
Watson	But you can't go underground.
Holmes	Curses!
Watson	Think, Holmes.
Holmes	I know what I'll do. I'll train everybody to run twenty six miles.
Watson	A marathon?
Holmes	No, I would prefer a Mars. I don't like peanuts.

The chimes of Big Ben are heard

Watson	Listen. Big Ben.
Holmes	Quick, hide. He may beat us up.
Watson	No, Holmes, the clock. The symbol of London Town. You must save the city, Holmes.
Holmes	I am beaten, Watson.
Narrator	Dick Whittington comes in. He is not carrying a cat.
Dick	I am Dick Whittington, Lord Mayor of London.
Holmes	Where's your cat?
Dick	I didn't bring him because he hasn't shaved.
Holmes	Why not?
Dick	Because eight out of ten cats prefer whiskers.
Narrator	We are sorry about the old jokes but we have to fill up the page somehow.
Dick	Will you save London, Holmes?
Holmes	No.
Dick	I offer you money.

Holmes	Of course I'll save London.
Dick	Here is five pounds on account.
Holmes	Can I have it on a cheque? Counts are normally villains.
Dick	Then here is a cheque, mate.
Holmes	That is the end of the game then. And so to bed.
Narrator	You cannot go to bed at this stage in the plot.
Watson	Holmes, don't just sit there with your hands in your pockets.
Holmes	These pockets are the key.
Watson	No, they're not the key. That's in the door. You told me to . . .
Holmes	No, you fool, the key to the mystery. What do you see now?
Watson	A hole.
Holmes	Exactly. And now I turn it inside out.
Watson	It's not a hole.
Holmes	Exactly. Moriarty has turned the holes inside out.
Watson	And we only have to turn them back again.
Holmes	Elementary, my dear Watson.
Watson	Elementary, my dear Holmes.
Narrator	And so London was saved. The fog was cleared. And here are Holmes and Watson leaving 221B Baker Street.
Holmes	Ah! Help!
Watson	Ah! Help!
Narrator	You've guessed it. They tripped over a cat and fell into a hole left by the Council.

4 The Terrible Ballad of the Chelsea Supporter

An octologue: a monologue for eight readers

Most people like a good poem, but I guarantee you can't get worse verse than this. Score ten out of ten if you can give one reason why it wasn't written by the Poet Laureate.

Characters	Reader 1
	Reader 2
	Reader 3
	Reader 4
	Reader 5
	Reader 6
	Reader 7
	Reader 8

Reader 1   The night was dark and stormy.

Reader 2   A boy stood in the street.

Reader 3   His soulful eyes were full of tears

Reader 4   And his boots were full of feet.

Reader 5   Bob stood there in that weather.

Reader 6   His cheeks were getting wet.

Reader 7   Because he'd got no trousers on.

Reader 8   He'd lost them in a bet.

Reader 1   His mother was at the window.

Reader 2   Her face was grey and thin.

Reader 3	But the silly old bat should've been fat
Reader 4	She was so full of gin.
Reader 5	'Oh do not leave your mother!'
Reader 6	Heartrending was her cry.
Reader 7	'Who'll strap on me wooden leg
Reader 8	Or put in me glass eye?'
Reader 1	He said: 'I needs must leave you
Reader 2	To seek work in London town.'
Reader 3	She said: 'You had better hurry
Reader 4	For your pants are falling down.'
Reader 5	He strode off round the corner
Reader 6	And borrowed some jeans from a tramp.
Reader 7	They were two sizes too small for him
Reader 8	And they gave him terrible cramp.
Reader 1	His mother tottered after him.
Reader 2	The lightning flashed like hell.
Reader 3	It was easy to get on his trail.
Reader 4	She had only to follow the smell.
Reader 5	He stood thumbing on the highway.
Reader 6	He stood there in the hail.
Reader 7	If his mother had used Persil
Reader 8	He could've gone by British Rail.
Reader 1	He was picked up by a truck driver.
Reader 2	A man with arms like steel.
Reader 3	But when they punctured in the rain
Reader 4	He made Bob change the wheel.
Reader 5	The city was not paved with gold
Reader 6	Just litter and old crisp bags.

Reader 7	The only gold that he could see
Reader 8	Was an empty packet of fags.
Reader 1	They arrived in early morning.
Reader 2	He was put off at King's Cross.
Reader 3	When he bent to pick a fag-end up,
Reader 4	He was kicked by a guardsman's hoss.
Reader 5	That kick put him in hospital.
Reader 6	He lay there feeling ill.
Reader 7	The doctor said: 'Just a bump on the head.
Reader 8	Give him a laxative pill.'
Reader 1	They shoved him from his sick bed
Reader 2	Before he could hardly walk.
Reader 3	He was so hungry he could eat
Reader 4	A plate of chips and the knife and fork.
Reader 5	But he got a job washing dishes.
Reader 6	He had to dry the plates.
Reader 7	If he was good, they gave him some pud
Reader 8	And the peelings off the tates.
Reader 1	But things were looking up for him.
Reader 2	Getting better by the hour.
Reader 3	They were looking up so well in fact
Reader 4	He could see the top of the Post Office Tower.
Reader 5	He went down to Stamford Bridge
Reader 6	Which is where Chelsea play.
Reader 7	They even put the floodlights on
Reader 8	So the 'skins' could fight night and day.
Reader 1	He became a Chelsea supporter.
Reader 2	He went to every match.

Reader 3	He became known as 'Pirate Bob'
Reader 4	'Cos he wore his Mum's eye-patch.
Reader 5	He went all the way to Moscow,
Reader 6	To Paris and Madrid.
Reader 7	If he'd have stayed at Gatwick,
Reader 8	He'd have saved himself five hundred quid.
Reader 1	He went up to a policeman
Reader 2	Dressed all in his leather.
Reader 3	He waited till the cop turned round
Reader 4	Then he hit him with a feather.
Reader 5	The cop was very mad at this.
Reader 6	He took him off to jail.
Reader 7	The magistrate said: 'What a dreadful crime!
Reader 8	You cannot have bail.'
Reader 1	He sat there in the prison.
Reader 2	He wished he had stuck with his Mum.
Reader 3	When he got up the chair did too
Reader 4	For he'd sat in some chewing gum.
Reader 5	Then he came up before the judge
Reader 6	Who said: 'What a terrible lout!
Reader 7	You can tell he's got a criminal mind
Reader 8	For his vest's on inside out!'
Reader 1	From the back of the court there came a cry.
Reader 2	Then up stomped young Bob's mum.
Reader 3	The judge gave a yell: 'It's the long-lost gel
Reader 4	I left on the Isle of Rhum!'
Reader 5	She said: 'Do not be hard on him.
Reader 6	Don't blame him for what he has done.'

Reader 7	She winked and her glass eye fell out.
Reader 8	'He really is your son!'
Reader 1	He said: 'Don't worry, Gladys.
Reader 2	I will treat him proper.
Reader 3	I declare him innocent
Reader 4	And it's six months for the copper.'
Reader 5	They sailed away into the sunset.
Reader 6	Then crash! The ship went down.
Reader 7	But they all clung to her wooden leg.
Reader 8	You didn't think we could let them drown!

5 Channel No. 5

Fed up with boring lessons? Watching TV is much better. Take a trip round the world with the new Channel No. 5.

Characters	Actor
	Actress
	Newscaster 1
	Newscaster 2
	Reporter 1
	Reporter 2
	Mr Scroggins
	Mrs Wood
	Young fellow from Crewe
	Girl
	Aussie
	Elephant

1 *A television studio*

A cardboard cut-out of Big Ben appears

Actor	Boing! Boing! Boing! Boing!
Actress	Boing! Boing! Boing! Boing!
Actor	Boing! Boing! Boing! Boing!
Actress	Boing! Boing! Boing! Boing!
Actor	*(Slowly)* Boing! Boing! Boing! Boing! Boing!
Newscaster 1	This is Channel number 5. The channel that is hot on the scent of the latest news. Here is the six o'clock news.
Actor	Sorry. Boing!
Newscaster 2	And here is our lead story. Today a man went to Blackpool and swallowed a one p piece, a two p piece, a five p piece and a ten p piece.

Reporter 1 Mr Scroggins today you came to Blackpool and swallowed a one p piece, a two p piece, a five p piece and a ten p piece.

Scroggins That is correct.

Reporter 1 Why did you do it?

Scroggins My doctor said the change would do me good.

Newscaster 1 Meanwhile back in the studio we have to report that:
There was a young fellow from Crewe
Went up Eiffel Tower for the view.
He fell from this height
But he was all right
For his braces caught on a screw.

Newscaster 2 Over to Paris.

Silence

Are you there, reporter?

Reporter 1 Just a minute, mate, it's a long way from Blackpool. I'm still swimming the Channel.

Newscaster 1 You must be wet.

Reporter 1 Yes, there's nothing wetter than Channel Four.

Newscaster 1 We seem to have a delay there. I'll go on to another piece of news. Over in Nuneaton we have a dog that thinks he's a tree.

Reporter 2 Now, Mrs Wood, how do you know that your dog thinks he's a tree?

Mrs Wood Well, he keeps going 'Bark! Bark! Bark!' all the time.

Reporter 2 I can't quite twig what you are saying.

Mrs Wood If he travels on the railway he always goes on a branch line.

Reporter 2 Ah now we're getting to the root of it.

Mrs Wood If he makes a telephone call it's always a trunk one.

Reporter 2 That's hardly fir.

Mrs Wood When I'm away he always pines for me.

Reporter 2	I'll be sycamore of this.
Mrs Wood	If he smokes he leaves ash all over the carpet. If he goes to football it's always to Nottingham Forest.
Reporter 2	Oakay, oakay, I think we had better leaf this. Over to Paris.
Reporter 1	Yes, here I am on top of the Eiffel Tower. The young fellow from Crewe is on his way up at the moment.
Actress	Boing!
Reporter 1	Can you talk me through what happened, please?
Fellow	I just lent over, mate, and . . .
Actress	Boing!
Reporter 1	He's going down again. I'll get him as he comes up. Ah!
Actress	Boing!
Reporter 1	Ah! Here he comes.
Fellow	Ah blur crab . . .
Reporter 1	I can't hear what you're saying. I'll just lean out a bit further. Just a bit further. Help! Hel . . .!
Newscaster 2	What's he doing? He must be insane.
Reporter 1	How did you guess? Yes, you are quite right I am in the Seine at the moment. Above me the Young Fellow from Crewe is still bouncing up and down. Back to the studio.
Newscaster 2	Our next piece of news comes from Australia.
Girl	Mum says will you bring home three fish and fifty pence worth of chips.
Newscaster 2	Yes, dear, but don't interrupt Daddy when he's at work . . .
Girl	She says make sure they're hot.
Newscaster 2	Go away, Maria. Sorry about that.

A phone rings

Excuse me. What? What? I wasn't rude to her. I know she's my daughter. Well, if you must be like that. Sorry. Over to Australia. Reports are coming in that kangaroos are jumping down not up. Over to Australia.

Reporter 2 I'm not there yet. I'm in Concorde, flying faster than the speed of sound. So you should not be able to hear me. So here's what I think of you and all the watching public: knickers, knickers, knickers!

Newscaster 1 What's he doing? I'm sorry, we'll go back to Australia later. Here in central London reports are coming in of a burst water main. It has flooded several important buildings *(gurgle)* of the capital *(gurgle)* and bloop argh! Where's my swimming costume? Over to *(gurgle)* Australia.

Reporter 2 I am now in Aussie land. All around me I can see men up to their necks in earth. I'll interview one of them. Why are you up to your neck in earth?

Aussie I've been jumped on by a kangaroo, mate.

Reporter 2 You're certainly down to earth about it.

Aussie It ain't fair dinkum is it, pom?

Reporter 2 Did you upset the kangaroo in any way?

Aussie 2 I did not, mate. It just jumped on me.

Actor Boing!

Reporter 2 Oh, I say, a kangaroo has just jumped on my head.

Actor Boing!

Reporter 2 I'm going down like a fence post.

Actor Boing!

Reporter 2 My chin is now level with the ground. So back to the . . . glug!

Newscaster 2 Here we are on an upper floor of the television studios. Reports are just coming in of a big fire in central London this afternoon. *(crackle)* It's getting a bit hot in here. If you don't mind, I'll take off my jacket. Seventeen appliances have been called out. Argh! Help!

A fire engine siren is heard briefly

Newscaster 1 Over in Burma we have news of elephants telling people jokes. Over to ... Help!

Reporter 1 I have just swum here from Paris. If you wait a minute while I get my breath back ... Ah, here is an elephant. Excuse me, Jumbo.

Elephant If you don't mind, my name is Cheryl.

Reporter 1 Cheryl, it has been reported that you elephants are telling people jokes.

Elephant That is correct.

Reporter 1 Would you tell one for the viewers, please?

Elephant A man walked down the road. He had jelly in one ear and custard in the other. I said to him: 'Why have you got jelly in one ear and custard in the other?' And he said: 'Speak up, mate, I'm a trifle deaf.'

Reporter 1 But that's a very old joke.

Elephant You don't expect an elephant to be original, do you? I say, fellows, have you heard what those kangaroos are doing to people in Australia ...?

Reporter 1 I'm getting out of here. Back to the studio.

Newscaster 1 Here we are in a tent in the grounds of the studios. Reports are just coming in that there has been trouble in the building of an underground railway in central London and ... *(creak)* Help!

Everything, including the cardboard cut-out of Big Ben, disappears.

6 Robin Hood and his Unmerrie Men

Down in ye olde Sherwood Forest in ye olden tymes things are not well. And it's not just the quarterstaffs that are striking, even the geese are complaining as well.

Characters	Narrator
	Little John, a dwarf
	Mutch the Miller
	Will Scarlet
	Maid Marian
	Friar Tuck, a monk
	Doctor Banajee
	Robin Hood
	Goose
	Blonde woman
	Buffet lady
	Station announcer
	King Richard
	Mark Spencer, a shoppe owner

1 *A forest glade*

Narrator   This tale is like the bell without a clapper: it has never been told. Long before the days of Brian Clough and Nottingham Forest, Robin Hood had a team called Sherwood Forest. But things were not going well and they were slipping down the first division league of robbers.

Little John   I'm fed up.

Mutch   Forsooth, I can't stand mutch more of this.

Will Scarlet   I'm very unchuffed. I mean all we ever do is rob, rob, rob.

Friar Tuck And now verily he wants us to do a night shift as well. I ask you.

Will Yes, Robin is certainly his name. Robin here and robin there. I'm worn out.

Maid Marian It's all right for you lot but I'm fed up cooking venison all day. Slaving over a hot cooking pot.

Mutch Yes, why can't we have some chips?

Maid Marian You can only have chips if Tuck helps me.

Mutch Why?

Maid Marian Because he's a good friar.

Robin Hood enters

Robin Men, the Sheriff of Nottingham approaches. Quick. To your posts.

Little John Verily we refuse!

Mutch We're on strike.

Robin But the only striking you can do is at the rich.

Will We won't budge till we get a thirty eight hour week and proper wine breaks.

Robin Who's the ring leader of this? I challenge him to a fight with quarterstaffs.

Little John The only quarter we're interested in, mate, is time and a quarter.

Mutch Yes, we want overtime.

Robin You louts! Look, you have Maid Marian cry.

Maid Marian It's not tears, you fool, it's steam from the cooking pot. I want help.

Friar Tuck Yes, we want some women.

Robin But you're supposed to be a monk.

Friar Tuck I may be a monk, but I won't be made a monkey of by you. Boo hoo!

The unmerrie men all cry

Maid Marian	They're sobbin', Robin, they're so depressed. Do something.
Robin	They'll have to see the doctor. I'll go to Nottingham and capture one.
Maid Marian	Why don't you go to the church and ring for one?
Robin	I don't like this new-fangled appointment system.

2 *The forest glade – later that day*

Little John	It's a woman doctor!
Maid Marian	Don't be a male chauvinist pig! This lady has come all the way from India to treat you.
Mutch	What's she going to treat us to? Sweets?
Maid Marian	To make you better, you fool.
Doctor	Say 'Ah!'
Men	Ah!
Doctor	Say 'one hundred and nine'.
Maid Marian	I thought it was ninety nine.
Doctor	Prince John has put VAT on it.
Men	One hundred and nine.
Doctor	Take off your Lincoln green.
Little John	I don't want her to see my bare skin.
Robin	She's not here to see your bear skin, you fool.
Doctor	*(to Tuck)* Take off that dirty habit.
Friar Tuck	Who's saying I've got a dirty habit?
Robin	Well, doctor.
Doctor	It could be.
Robin	Could be what?
Doctor	The well, you fool.
Robin	We don't use a well. We use crystal-clear stream water.

Doctor	But you forget you're always fighting in it in those dirty tights. I'll write you out a prescription. I'll just pluck a feather from this fat goose.
Goose	Squawk! I wish someone would invent the ballpoint pen!
Doctor	What your men really need is a holiday. They're out in the fresh air too much. They need a break in the town.
Robin	Right, men, we'll go to Nottingham and rob the castle.
Maid Marian	Not robin again. Can't we go to London to see the shoppes?
Robin	Prince John is in London. He'll put us in the Tower.
Mutch	The Post Office Tower?
Robin	The Tower of London, you fool.
Will	We can disguise ourselves as Nottingham Forest supporters.
Men	Yes!
Robin	All right, we'll take a trip by coach.
Little John	But this is the age of the mule train.
Robin	Very well, by train then. I only hope it's on time.

3 *Ye olde Grantham Station*

Maid Marian	What a boring place!
Blonde woman	Do you mind! I was born here.
Robin	Who are you?
Blonde woman	I'm a Thatcher.
Robin	Then buzz off and mend a few roofs.
Mutch	I didn't realise that we would have to change trains.
Will	Let's go to ye olde buffet for a drink of mead.
Buffet lady	No football supporters here.

Robin	We're not football supporters.
Buffet lady	Then why's he wearing a red shirt and scarf?
Robin	Because he's Will Scarlet.
Buffet lady	You look a rough lot to me. I'm serving no mead.
Little John	If you can't answer my riddle will you serve us?
Buffet lady	Oh I love riddles.
Little John	How do you make a football?
Buffet lady	Go on, how do you make a football?
Little John	Tread on its toes. Hee! Hee!
Buffet lady	Tee hee! What a merry jest!
Announcer	Hear ye! Hear ye! The next mule train arriving at Platform Two will be the ten of the clock for Doncaster and York.
Robin	Just look who's getting off!
Narrator	The National Anthem plays. All get up, please.
Little John	I'm still drinking me mead.
Narrator	Get up!
King Richard	I'm King Richard.
Mutch	Are you any relation to Cliff?
King Richard	Hello, Hood, I'm just back from Turkey.
Friar Tuck	Up the Reds!
King Richard	We certainly gave them a bashing. Ten nil. And we beat up ninety of their supporters.
Narrator	That should be one hundred. Prince John has put VAT on in your absence.
Robin	Yes, sire, he has cruelly taxed the poor.
King Richard	Has he? Then I'll send Blondel to sing to him. I can't think of a worse punishment than that. You should hear his latest LP.
Marian	LP?

King Richard	Lousy parrottings.
Announcer	Hear ye! Hear ye! The London train is delayed for three days plus VAT.
Robin	It's back to ye olde buffet, men. What are those custard pies for?
Narrator	Well I thought that if we could not think how to end the play we could throw them at each other. It would make a funny ending.
Friar Tuck	How corny can you get!
Mark Spencer	Just a minute. I own a chain of shoppes. Who made that green coat with the hood?
Robin	It was maid by Marian.
Mark Spencer	Do you know that you have invented the duffel coat and the anorak?
Marian	Have I?
Mark Spencer	I'll pay you ten thousand crowns for the patent.
Robin	I'll sign immediately. If only I had a pen.
Goose	I'm off.
Buffet lady	Use this one, duck.
Robin	Duck or goose, I don't mind.
Men	We're rich. We need never rob again.Three cheers for Marian and Robin.
Narrator	No, it's four cheers.
Men	We know: Prince John has put VAT on it!

7 The Parcel

It's nice to receive a parcel. But the Tompkins family are not very pleased with the parcel that gets stuck in their doorway. They are even less grateful when they find out what's in it.

Characters	Mr Tompkins
	Mrs Tompkins
	Anne-Marie
	Nigel
	Gran
	British Rail Man 1
	British Rail Man 2

---

1 *The Tompkins' house*

The doorbell rings

Mrs Tompkins	Go and answer the door, Anne-Marie. My hands are wet.
Anne-Marie	Can't Nigel go? I'm doing my nails.
Gran	I'll go.
Mrs Tompkins	Don't you get up from that chair too quick. You'll have one of your dizzy turns.
Nigel	I'll go. It might be the postman.
Anne-Marie	If it's Ted, tell him I won't be a minute.

Nigel opens the door

BR Man 1	British Rail parcels here. I've a parcel for the Tompkins family.
Nigel	That's us.
BR Man 2	Sign here, mate.

Nigel signs the form

Nigel	There you are.
BR Man 2	Thanks.
Nigel	But where's the parcel?
BR Man 1	It's outside on the grass. It's a bit big. Cheerio, mate.
Nigel	Hey, Mum, it's a big parcel.
Mrs Tompkins	Bring it in here, Nigel. My hands are wet.
Nigel	But it's about three metres long and a metre wide.
Mrs Tompkins	Stop playing your jokes, Nigel.
Anne-Marie	Is it Ted? Is that you, Ted?
Nigel	I'm not joking, Mum. I can't even lift up one end. It's ever so heavy.
Mrs Tompkins	I have to do everything in this house.
Gran	I'll lend a hand.
Mrs Tompkins	No, you won't, Gran. I don't want you lifting anything heavy or you'll have one of your dizzy turns. Anne-Marie, give our Nigel a hand.
Anne-Marie	What for?
Mrs Tompkins	Give me patience.

She comes to the door

	Oh, it is big! Who could have sent us that?
Nigel	It doesn't say. You get one end. I think we can wiggle it through the door.
Mrs Tompkins	I think we had better wait for your father.
Nigel	Come on, Mum, we can do it.

Gran appears at the door

Gran	What is it?

Mrs Tompkins	It's a big parcel, Gran. It's very heavy.
Gran	I'll help.
Mrs Tompkins	You go back to your chair. Anne-Marie!
Anne-Marie	Is it Ted?
Mrs Tompkins	Come and give us a hand with this parcel.
Anne-Marie	My nails are still wet.
Mrs Tompkins	Come on, Nigel. You go in. I'll push from out here. I'll have to watch my back. Now careful.
Nigel	It's moving. It's half in.
Mrs Tompkins	It's going to get stuck. It is stuck. Just what I needed when I'm getting ready for Christmas, too.
Anne-Marie	Nigel, Ted can't get in now.
Nigel	He can go round the back.
Anne-Marie	I'm not having Ted go to the back door. You really are the limit.
Gran	Can I open it?
Mrs Tompkins	Do go back to your chair, Gran. We've got it stuck. What shall we do?
Nigel	I could saw a bit out of the door frame.
Mrs Tompkins	I'm not having that.
	Mr Tompkins arrives
Mr Tompkins	Hello. Hello. What have we here?
Mrs Tompkins	Thank goodness you've come. This parcel is stuck in the door.
Mr Tompkins	No bother. I'll just get my body behind it. I wasn't a front-row forward for nothing.
Nigel	I'll climb out and shove as well.

Mr Tompkins	There, it's moving.
Nigel	Great!
Mr Tompkins	Yes, it's moving.
Mrs Tompkins	So is the door frame.
Mr Tompkins	Got it. It's in the hall.
Mrs Tompkins	So is the door frame and the front door.
Mr Tompkins	I'll put them back.
Mrs Tompkins	The door is under the parcel.
Mr Tompkins	It must be a Christmas present. I wonder who's sent it?
Mrs Tompkins	Let's open it and find out.
Mr Tompkins	We can't open it till December the twenty fifth.
Mrs Tompkins	But it's December the first. Are you going to leave it here till then?
Mr Tompkins	It's as good a place as any.
Mrs Tompkins	But we can't get up the stairs.
Mr Tompkins	We can climb over.
Mrs Tompkins	It's wedged right against the loo door. We must open it now. How can we get in the loo?
Gran	Oh, no. You can't open it till December the twenty fifth. We never did in the old days. It will spoil Christmas.

Mr Tompkins	Quite right, Gran.
Anne-Marie	You must open it. How can Ted get in the front door?
Nigel	There is no front door to get in.
Mr Tompkins	If I prop it up, I can get the front door out. Then we can crawl underneath it to get to the loo.
Mrs Tompkins	Do you think I'm crawling under that for four weeks? And what about Gran?
Gran	I don't mind. It'll be exciting. I do love a surprise. I wonder what's in it for me?
Mrs Tompkins	Crawling under there would give you a dizzy turn. Nigel, open it now. I insist!
Gran	Spoilsport.

Nigel takes the wrapping off the parcel

Nigel	There's a wooden box under this paper. I'll need a screwdriver and a hammer.
Mr Tompkins	They're in that cupboard under the stairs.
Nigel	It's blocking that cupboard under the stairs.
Mr Tompkins	Then it'll have to go out again.
Mrs Tompkins	After all that trouble we had to get it in.
Mr Tompkins	No trouble. Right, Nigel, shove.
Nigel	Right.
Mr Tompkins	There it's out enough.
Mrs Tompkins	You've bent the radiator.
Mr Tompkins	It can be unbent.

Mrs Tompkins	But it's dripping.
Mr Tompkins	Don't start finding me jobs now, dear. Get the hammer and screwdriver, Nigel.
Nigel	Got them.
Mr Tompkins	Now help me push it in again.
Mrs Tompkins	You could open it outside.
Mr Tompkins	You don't open Christmas presents in the garden.
Gran	What a silly idea.
Mrs Tompkins	I only thought that . . .
Gran	Don't you be a spoilsport. It's bad enough opening it now.
Mr Tompkins	Push, Nigel.
Nigel	Right.
Mr Tompkins	There it's in again.
Mrs Tompkins	You've ripped the carpet.
Mr Tompkins	Just a little snag.
Mrs Tompkins	If you call sixty centimetres a snag.
Nigel	I can't wait to see what's inside.
Gran	You should be waiting for December the twenty fifth. Not like the old days.
Nigel	There, that's the lid off. I say. It's well wrapped up.
Mr Tompkins	Let me see.

Nigel	No, I can do it. I say . . .
Mrs Tompkins	What is it?
Nigel	It's a gorilla.
	Mrs Tompkins screams
	It's all right. I don't think it's alive.
Gran	Let me look. Oh!
Mrs Tompkins	She's had one of her dizzy turns.
Mr Tompkins	What'd she do that for? It's only a stuffed one. It's not alive.
Mrs Tompkins	Who would send us a stuffed gorilla? Ugh!
Mr Tompkins	Let me stand it up. Nigel, give me a hand.
Mrs Tompkins	Shouldn't you be giving Gran a hand?
Mr Tompkins	She'll be all right. She's on the carpet. I want to see it out of the box.
Mrs Tompkins	Anne-Marie, get Gran a glass of water and her tablets.
Anne-Marie	I've got to get changed for Ted. How can I get up the stairs with that standing there?
Mrs Tompkins	We must get rid of it. It doesn't go with the wallpaper.
Mr Tompkins	But it's a present. We might offend someone.
Nigel	Let's put it in the front room window. It'll frighten the burglars away.
Mr Tompkins	What a good idea.
Anne-Marie	I take Ted in the front room. I'm not sharing him with a gorilla.

Gran	*(coming round)* What happened?
Nigel	It's only a gorilla, Gran.
Gran	A gorilla! Oh!
	She faints again
Mrs Tompkins	Now she's fainted again. Will you please get on to somebody and find out who it belongs to?
Mr Tompkins	It was addressed to us. It must be ours.
Mrs Tompkins	I know it was addressed to us. But it can't belong to us. Get on the phone to British Rail at once.
Mr Tompkins	Oh, all right. We'll offend someone. Where is the phone?
Nigel	It's under its foot. I'll lift it.
Gran	Where am I?
Mrs Tompkins	It's all right, Gran. It's only stuffed.
Nigel	Just a little bit more.
Gran	It's not stuffed. It's moving.
	She faints again
Nigel	Here's the phone.
	Mr Tompkins dials
Mr Tompkins	British Rail? No, I don't want the times of the trains. I've got a stuffed gorilla here. No, I'm not playing games. I want to know who sent it. What? He's rung off.
Mrs Tompkins	Give me the phone. What's the number?
Mr Tompkins	66437.
	She dials
Mrs Tompkins	British Rail. Will you please come and take away this stuffed gorilla. What? You've had a man on the phone. It might be one of a pair. You fool! That was my

husband. What? Try the museum. He says try the museum.

Mr Tompkins dials again

Mr Tompkins Is that the museum? This is Mr Tompkins, 7 Cranley Gardens. We've got a stuffed gorilla here. Has it got a what? A white spot under its chin? Nigel, look and see if it's got a white spot under its chin.

Nigel It has.

Mr Tompkins It has. Oh. Oh. I see.

He puts down the phone

It should have gone to the museum. It's a computer error.

Nigel What a pity. I rather fancied having a stuffed gorilla. What's for tea, Mum?

Mrs Tompkins Stuffed pork. I was going to gorilla it. I mean grill it. I don't know what I do mean. It keeps looking at me.

Anne-Marie Clean up this mess, Mum. Ted'll be here in a minute. Look at all this paper.

She kicks it

Mrs Tompkins Careful. Your Gran's under there. These computers!

2 *The Tompkins' house – the next day*

The doorbell rings

Mrs Tompkins Answer the door, Anne-Marie.

Anne-Marie I can't. I'm putting in my earrings. Can't Nigel go?

Mrs Tompkins Really, Anne-Marie, I've not slept a wink all night with there being no front door. Nigel! Nigel! Where is he? If you want something done, do it yourself.

She opens the door

BR Man 1 We've come to take away one stuffed gorilla.

Mrs Tompkins	Thank goodness for that. Now we can put our door back on.
BR Man 1	No trouble, missus. We'll soon have it out.
Mrs Tompkins	The crate as well.
BR Man 2	Right, missus. Over to your left, Bert.
Gran	Are they getting that beastly thing out of the house?
Mrs Tompkins	Yes, Gran.
Gran	I shall never be the same again. What a turn I had.
Anne-Marie	Is that Ted?
Mrs Tompkins	No, it's the gorilla men.
Gran	What, the gorilla again?
Mrs Tompkins	Go and sit down.
BR Man 2	Up a bit.
BR Man 1	Right, mate.
	There is a crash
BR Man 2	Oh, sorry about that mirror.
Gran	The mirror! We'll have seven years' bad luck.
Mrs Tompkins	This family never has anything else. Just get it out.
BR Man 1	Right, there we are. We'll take it to the van now.
Mrs Tompkins	Am I glad to see the back of that. These computers!
BR Man 2	As you say, missus, these computers. Just sign here. Thank you.
Gran	It's gone very dark in here. I can't see out of the windows.
Mrs Tompkins	Don't be silly, Gran, it's morning.

BR Man 1   We've put the stuffed kangaroo, the Roman bath, the Egyptian mummy case, the dinosaur skeleton and the African pots in the back garden.

Mrs Tompkins   You what?

BR Man 2   Come on, Bert.

Nigel rushes in

Nigel   Mum, there's a whole line of trucks queuing down the road with parcels for us.

Mrs Tompkins   Oh, no!

8 Quick Promotion

In these days of high unemployment it is not easy to get a job, never mind promotion. But Mr Rumble, a teacher, goes from being unemployed to the position of Headmaster in an afternoon.

Characters	Mr Rumble
	Boy
	Girl
	Voice/woman
	Vera, secretary
	Mr Higginbottom, Headmaster
	Cook
	Felicity
	Miss Simpkins

1 *At the end of the drive to Meadowbank Academy*

Mr Rumble What a hot day! Two miles walk from the station. I wonder why I wasn't picked up by car. Ah, here we are: Meadowbank Academy for Young Ladies and Gentlemen. Headmaster Mr I T Higginbottom M A. This could be my first teaching job. What are that young boy and girl doing chasing a sheep?

Boy Corner it.

Girl Lovely grub.

Mr Rumble I say, what are you doing?

Girl We're getting our dinner.

Mr Rumble Ha! Ha! Where will I find Mr Higginbottom?

Boy At the races, I expect.

Mr Rumble Ah, he's keen on horses.

Boy I'll say. He's a bookie.

Mr Rumble	I must say I'm going to enjoy the sense of humour in this place. The Head a bookie. Ha! Ha!
Girl	Try that bell over there.

Mr Rumble walks down a driveway and over a bridge to a castle-like door. He rings the bell

Voice	Are you from the Income Tax?
Mr Rumble	No.
Voice	The Press?
Mr Rumble	No.
Voice	You're not Plain Clothes, are you?
Mr Rumble	No, I'm Wilfred Rumble. I've come about the teaching post.

A woman opens a heavy door

Woman	Oh, you're the suck . . . I mean, gentleman. Put up your arms while I frisk you.
Mr Rumble	Frisk me?
Woman	We can't be too careful, mate. We have some rich kids in here. You might be a kidnapper.
Mr Rumble	Oh, very wise of you.
Woman	Sorry about the car. The boys went out on a job in it.
Mr Rumble	Working?
Woman	You could call it that.
Mr Rumble	Just the day for it.
Woman	This hot weather brings out the traffic. Could affect the getaway.
Mr Rumble	The getaway?
Woman	Yes, when they get away from work. You'd better come and meet the boss . . . er, Headmaster.

2 *The secretary's office*

Woman	Hello, Vera, a jer . . . gentleman to see the boss.
Vera	I'll see if Mr Higginbottom is free.
Woman	Of course he's free. He's been out two years.
Vera	That's the proper thing a secretary says.

She goes in

Oh, Larry, stop it. No, Larry! Don't do that.

She comes out red-faced

Mr Higginbottom will see you now, Mr Rumble.

3 *The Head's office*

Mr Higginbottom is a small man with greasy hair, smoking a big cigar. He has a bright yellow tie and a black shirt

Mr Higgin-bottom	Come in, Rumble. Sit down. You weren't followed, were you?
Mr Rumble	Er no.
Mr Higgin-bottom	You can't be too careful. I'll close the curtains. Drink?
Mr Rumble	I'd like a cup of tea.
Mr Higgin-bottom	I said a drink. How many fingers of whisky do you take?
Mr Rumble	Er, fingers?
Mr Higgin-bottom	I can't stand a man who can't take a drink.
Mr Rumble	Oh, a big one.
Mr Higgin-bottom	That's the spirit, Rumble. I'm glad you applied for this post. Now versatility is what I'm after.

Cook rushes in

Cook	The little creeps . . . *(sees Rumble)* . . . er dears, want dinner again.

Mr Higgin-bottom	But they had dinner yesterday.
Cook	That's what I told them.
Mr Higgin-bottom	Pick out the Oliver Twists and put them in the cool ... er, the cool classroom and give them what they deserve.
	Cook goes
	Constant problems on this job, Rumble. You're sure you weren't followed.
Mr Rumble	No.
Mr Higgin-bottom	Good. Now what subjects can you offer?
Mr Rumble	RE.
Mr Higgin-bottom	What's that?
Mr Rumble	Religious Education.
Mr Higgin-bottom	Ah, nothing like religion.
Mr Rumble	I'm rather good on the Bible.
Mr Higgin-bottom	What's that?
Mr Rumble	The Bible. The good book.
Mr Higgin-bottom	I like a good read. Does it have a happy ending?
Mr Rumble	Well, it is full of good news.
Mr Higgin-bottom	News? Keep out of newspapers, Rumble. They uncover all sorts of things about you. No, what I mean by religion is can you teach the children to dress up as vicars and things?
Mr Rumble	Dress up as vicars?
Mr Higgin-bottom	Yes, it's very useful. I once sold Westminster Abbey to an American dressed up as a bishop.
Mr Rumble	Oh, really, sir, your sense of humour. Ha! Ha!

Mr Higgin-bottom	Quite. Now, what about Maths?
Mr Rumble	I can do Modern Maths.
Mr Higgin-bottom	Good. If I had a crossed double at Newmarket at twelve to one against and seven to four on, how much would I get?
Mr Rumble	I would leave it to the bookmaker.
Mr Higgin-bottom	Never trust a bookmaker. You wouldn't want to send a boy or girl out into the wide world to be swindled by bookies, would you?
Mr Rumble	Er . . . no.
Mr Higgin-bottom	That's what I mean by Modern Maths.
	Vera comes in
Vera	Felicity insists on seeing you, Larr . . . sir.
Mr Higgin-bottom	I'm very busy.
Felicity	*(rushing in)* I got wet in bed when it rained last night.
Mr Higgin-bottom	Just dew, Felicity. Just dew.
Felicity	But I was soaked.
Mr Higgin-bottom	That's living in the country. It'll help your swimming, dear. You know your Mum pays extra for swimming lessons.
Felicity	I'll spill the beans on this place.
Mr Higgin-bottom	Now that would be very unwise, Felicity.
Felicity	Oh, all right.
	She goes
Mr Higgin-bottom	Vera, how much did we get for that lead?
Vera	Twenty pounds a ton.

Mr Higgin-bottom	Buy a bit back. Offer them twenty one. We may need a box and some cement for Felicity. Sculpture you know, Rumble.
	Vera goes
Mr Rumble	Oh, yes.
Mr Higgin-bottom	How is your Art, Rumble. Can you draw ten-pound notes?
Mr Rumble	Only from the bank. Ha! Ha!
Mr Higgin-bottom	I'll have to teach you. The last bloke we had made big money.
Mr Rumble	That was good.
Mr Higgin-bottom	No, it was bad. It was a centimetre too big.
	Miss Simpkins rushes in
Miss Simpkins	I'm afraid the still ... er, alcohol machine has been broken.
Mr Higgin-bottom	Oh, and which little creep did that?
Miss Simpkins	Well, Jones Major has difficulty in walking, sir.
Mr Higgin-bottom	The poor boy. Send him to the medical room immediately. I'll visit him there.
	She goes
	A devoted chemistry mistress, Rumble. Just another little problem. Now what about Geography?
Mr Rumble	I can read a map.
Mr Higgin-bottom	You could plan the quickest route to Spain or South America then. That could be very useful. I'm warming to you. Now History.
Mr Rumble	I know about the Greeks.
Mr Higgin-bottom	Do you! There are some tough boys in that mob. Could be useful. Now Sport.
Mr Rumble	I can referee rugger.

Mr Higgin-bottom	We go in more for athletics here. Like how to run a hundred metres carrying a heavy object.
Mr Rumble	A shot?
Mr Higgin-bottom	*(ducking)* I didn't hear anything.
Mr Rumble	No, I mean putting the shot.
Mr Higgin-bottom	You had me frightened for a minute. No, I mean carrying something like a safe, just as an example. Now English.
Mr Rumble	I'm quite good at that.
Mr Higgin-bottom	Good. Then perhaps you could look over this letter to me from the Tax Office. They don't believe I run this place at a loss. You must write the reply.

Vera rushes in

Vera	The Fuzz are coming up the drive.
Mr Higgin-bottom	I've got to go.
Mr Rumble	But what about the job?
Mr Higgin-bottom	I'll tell you what. I'll make you Headmaster till the heat's off.
Mr Rumble	Till the heat's off?
Mr Higgin-bottom	Till the weather cools down. Put on these glasses. Stick this cigar in your mouth. Remember you are Higgin-bottom. Just stall for twenty minutes. Come on, Vera.

Mr Rumble sits in the Headmaster's chair and leans back

Mr Rumble	Just think! Me a headmaster! I never dreamed I would get promotion so quickly.

Mr Higginbottom and Vera open the bookcase and disappear down a flight of steps.

Activities

What's the joke?

Chemistry Lesson

> How do you count after ten?
> You could take a shoe off, sir.

> What is the best conductor?
> Copper, sir.
> The police! I didn't do it.
> I swear I am innocent.

The case of the missing Holes

> Listen. Big Ben.
> Quick, hide. He may beat us up.

> You just need a shave, Holmes.
> Ha! I only did it to razor laugh.

> It's only the door. Answer it.
> But it hasn't spoken to me.

* Make a list of all the 'silly jokes' you can find in the plays. Which are your favourites?

* Tell each other any silly jokes like these that you know. Practise them in pairs. Then present them to the rest of the class.

Channel No. 5

If he makes a telephone call it's always a trunk one.
That's hardly fir.
When I'm away he always pines for me.
I'll be sycamore of this.

Robin Hood and his Unmerrie Men

Robin is certainly his name.
Robin here and robin there.

How do you make a football?
Tread on its toes.

You can only have chips if Tuck helps me.
Why?
Because he's a good friar.

* Make a Joke Book. Start off by writing in ones from the play.
  Try to collect: cracker jokes
                    funny graffiti
                    knock knock jokes
                    elephant jokes.

* Choose your favourite jokes and draw some cartoons to go with them.

Act out
Use a cassette-recorder

1 You take part in a bank raid with Louie and his gang that goes terribly and amusingly wrong. Act out the scene.

2 One of your science lessons at school ends in disaster. Act out the lesson and its final moments.

3 Act out another day-in-the-life of Watson and Holmes at 221B Baker Street. Remember that Moriarty is always trying to outwit them . . . .

4 What is it like being a reporter for Channel No. 5? (It could be the first smellyvision.) Present a location report that goes wrong.

5 One day Prince John meets Robin Hood and his band. Act out the scene.

6 What happens when the *next* round of parcels arrive at the Tompkins' house? Act out the events.

7 Imagine your own school is like Meadowbank Academy. Act out some scenes based on your own teachers and friends in your class.

Make your play lively and fun to act.
When you have worked at it, write out the script neatly.
Try it out. Tape it. Play it to the group.
Make a programme and a poster for your play.
Give it a good title.

Write on

1 *The Bank Raid* takes some 'leaps in time' between scenes. Write some dialogue which might have taken place between any of the characters during one of these time leaps.

2 Imagine Dr Batty has started at his new job, leading a scientific project. Write a letter from his new employer to the headmaster, reporting on how Dr Batty is doing.

3 Watson and Holmes work closely together as a partnership. Write a story or short script about two other characters who works as partners.

4 Write your own mystery story with Watson and Holmes coming along to solve the mystery.

5 Write your own 'Terrible Ballad'. Work with a partner and try to make the ballad scan and rhyme.

6 Invent Channel 6. How would it be different from the television channels we already have and from Channel No. 5?

7 Robin Hood faces a most unlikely kind of strike from his men. Write your own story of a strike in an unusual situation.

8 Robin Hood stole from the rich and gave to the poor. Imagine what would happen if a modern-day hero were to do the same. Write the hero's or heroine's diary for a week.

9 Write a scene which happens either before or after *Quick Promotion*.

Be a designer

1 Choose any four characters from the 'Eight Even Sillier Plays'. Draw/paint their portraits. Compare your pictures with others in your group. Put together a 'rogues gallery' from the plays.

2 Design a funny poster to advertise any of the plays.

3 Draw a scene from *one* of the plays. If you plan on performing one of the scripts, design a stage set.

4 Design and draw some funny costumes for any of the characters in the plays.

Write a silly play

Make plans

* What is your play going to be about? Give it a good title.

* How many people are going to be in the play?

* Think of some amusing names for your characters.

* Where is the action going to take place?

a classroom	a café
a park	around the dinner-table
on a bus	a courtroom

* How many different scenes will there be? Or will the action be in one place only?

* What time of the day, week, or year is your play set?

* If you aim to perform your play to an audience, you will need:

sets	costumes
lighting	music
props	sound effects.

Writing

* Think of some bright, eye-catching lines to start your play. Readers will only want to read on if the opening lines grab their attention. Think about how these eight plays begin. Do they catch your attention?

* Write dialogue that is lively and perhaps funny. It must also be true-to-life. Good dialogue does two things at once:
  a It tells you about characters and why people in the play are behaving as they are.
  b It moves the story along in an interesting way.

* Vary the length of speeches.
  Short ones are usually best if you are trying to write a quick-moving play.
  Longer speeches are often kept for important moments.

* Decide how many stage directions you need.
  Too *few* – and it will make the play difficult to act out.
  Too *many* – and the reader will get confused and bored.

* If you are writing a play with several scenes, complete *one* at a time. It is a good idea to give each scene-ending the sort of line that leaves the audience or the reader wondering just what *is* going to happen next.

* Now try to write another kind of play. Use these ideas to help you.

Get it right

All writers draft out more than one version before writing the final play. When you have completed your FIRST DRAFT, read it through with a friend.

* What parts can be improved?
* Are there any lines or jokes which don't sound right?
* Should any characters be taken out or added?
* Can the scene-endings be more interesting or exciting?

Now work on your SECOND (and third) DRAFT.

Remember who will be watching your play.

Your written play must be polished and ready for your actors to read in a group. Make sure that the words *sound* right when you hear them.

Final draft

Write the play out neatly, with plenty of space on the page, so that others can read it easily.
Make sure the names of the characters are printed clearly in the margin.
Perhaps your teacher can photocopy it for class reading?

Even once it has been read you may like to rewrite parts to make it better. Professional writers go on rewriting their plays while they are in rehearsal – and some even go on doing this once a play has opened in the theatre.

Good luck with your writing!